Succeed as a
new manager

How to inspire your team
and be a great boss

A & C B

© A & C Black Publishers Ltd 2006

First published in 2006 by
A & C Black Publishers Ltd
38 Soho Square
London W1D 3HB

British Library Cataloguing in Publication Data
A CIP record for this book is available from the British Library.

ISBN–10: 0–7136–7524–1
ISBN–13: 978–0–7136–7524–5

Design by Fiona Pike, Pike Design, Winchester
Typeset by RefineCatch Limited, Bungay, Suffolk
Printed in Italy by Legoprint

A & C Black uses paper produced with elemental chlorine-free pulp, harvested from managed sustainable forests.

Contents

How do you rate as a new manager?

Answer the questions and work out your score, then read the guidance points.

How do you feel about your new role?
a) Terrified!
b) Excited–I feel ready for my new role.
c) Very confident; I've waited a long time for this.

Have you made any decisions about your management style?
a) I don't plan on acting any differently.
b) I'll be friendly and approachable.
c) I'll treat colleagues very differently as they will be working *for* me, not with me.

How do you feel about managing people older than you?
a) I worry about my lack of experience.
b) I don't see that age is an issue.
c) It's not a problem.

Be truthful! Out of 10, how do you rate your listening skills?
a) 4–6
b) 7–10
c) 1–3

How often do you say 'thank you'?
a) Too much!
b) Regularly.
c) Not very often.

What is your view on conflict?
a) I avoid it if at all possible.
b) Sometimes it's unavoidable.
c) I don't have a problem with it!

Which of the below is closest to your style of communication?
a) Passive.
b) Assertive.
c) Aggressive.

How do you view delegation?
a) I see it as laziness. If a job comes to you, you should deal with it yourself.
b) An important process for developing both yourself and your staff.
c) Very handy–if you don't want to do something, pass it on!

How do you feel about your managers?
a) I worry that they don't think much of me.
b) I respect their experience. We're all on the same team.
c) I don't think much of them, so try to avoid them and get on with my job.

a = 1, b = 2, and c = 3.
Now add up your scores.

■**9–14:** Now you have had the good news it's important to build up your confidence, reminding yourself that your company has chosen to promote you. If they believe in you there's no reason why you shouldn't! Read chapter **1** to give you a head start. To avoid getting bogged down in detail, you mustn't be afraid to delegate–chapter **5** will give you some pointers, and chapter **7** will help you manage your personal workload.

■**15–21:** You clearly have a balanced approach to your new role, but don't underestimate the change this will cause in your working relationships. Remember to keep a professional distance. Chapters **3** and **4** will help you to feel at home as a manager. Building teams is a new skill for you to learn–read all about it in chapter **2**.

■**22–27:** Remember that overconfidence can be a problem too! You are in danger of damaging relationships through your perceived arrogance. Listening and 'bonding' are very important skills for managers–read chapters **4** and **6** for advice on positive management.

Whatever your score, remember that as your role grows so should your contacts list. Chapter **8** will help you build a network of mutually valuable contacts.

Settling into your new job

Congratulations! Your promotion campaign has been successful and you're now a manager. You're likely to be responsible for managing a team of up to 15 people, either in a company you already work for, or in a new organisation. This is obviously very exciting for you, though you may feel a bit daunted at the prospect, especially if you were previously a member of the team you will now be managing.

However, provided you follow a few basic rules, there is no reason why such fears can't easily be overcome, and your new role will give you excellent scope to stretch your wings and fulfil your potential. This chapter will give you these basic rules and help to smooth the path forward into this new phase of your working life.

Step one: Think about some key questions

1 I'm worried I might not be up to the job. How can I overcome my nerves?

It's only natural to have some feelings along these lines, and most people do when faced with a new challenge. Try to keep your worries under control, though, as a crisis of confidence may affect your chance of success. Keep positive and remind yourself of your skills and competence to do the job—after all, the company has recognised them, otherwise you wouldn't have been offered the role! Look after your health too: make sure you get plenty of sleep and exercise, so you feel fighting fit and ready to take on anything.

2 Is it likely that my new job will affect my home life?

Almost certainly, yes. Moving into any new job can be stressful, and even more so when new or extra levels of responsibility are involved. The trick is to make sure you're prepared for it, and face the fact that your life may be more demanding than ever before. Talk this over with your family and friends at an early stage; it will be a huge help if they are ready to lend their support while you get to grips with your new role, and also keep 'home' distractions to a minimum as you're settling in so that you can focus.

3 Will I need to change my persona at work?

No, not essentially, but you may need to adjust your attitude and the way you think about your job. A lot of management is about standing back from the detail and seeing the 'big picture' of what is happening so that you can make strategic decisions about how to act. Rather than getting involved in the nitty-gritty of individual tasks (as you may have done as a team member), try to take an objective overview. If you can learn to see the wood for the trees, you'll naturally behave in a way that suits the circumstances.

Step two: Research and plan your new job

First things first: if you're moving to a new company to take up your job, find out everything possible about it, the department or section you'll be in, the job itself, and anything else you can think of.

If you're moving up the ranks at your current place of work, you'll know much of this already, but, whatever the situation, don't prejudge what you're going to find and don't be bound by what you've done before or how any of your previous employers operated.

From all this information, try to form at least a tentative plan in advance—it's much harder to do this once you're in the post. For example, what do you want to achieve? How might you need to develop yourself to match the new demands? Think honestly about your strengths and weaknesses: how can you use your qualities and experience to their best advantage and compensate for your limitations?

TOP TIP
If possible, you could make some discreet
inquiries about your predecessor: why he or
she left, what management style they
preferred, how people responded to that,
what may need to be changed, and so on.
Again, if you're not moving companies you
may know some of this already, but try to
take a more balanced view of things and try to
see things from the other person's
perspective too.

Step three: Engage with your team

Once you start your new job, make this your first priority. You
need to know:

- the purpose of your department, team, or unit and its
  goals
- the work being done
- the current state of play
- any customer expectations that need to be met

Get all your team members together as soon as possible to
introduce yourself, and then arrange meetings with each of
them individually. Keep these meetings as friendly and
informal as you can, but allow a generous amount of time
and plan some kind of framework for the discussion. Listen
carefully to what people have to say, and get information

about them as individuals. Most importantly, ask each person the question: what should I do or not do to help you perform your job effectively?

TOP TIP

Listening—and tuning in properly—to your team's concerns is a key part of your early days in a new job. That doesn't mean for a moment that you should promise them the moon, but simply that you'll be in a much better position to represent those concerns to your own managers. You need to be able to fight your team's corner.

Step four: Plan some 'quick wins'

Next, plan a few targets that you can hit quickly and easily, all of which will help you to feel more at home and on top of things. Achieving these also eases the pressure you feel to perform and create a positive first impression and begins the relationship-building process. Quick wins might include things like familiarising yourself with systems or ways of working if you're new to the company (for example, the internal e-mail system); setting up an early discussion with your line manager, arranging introductory meetings with suppliers or customers (external and internal), or even taking your team to the pub one lunchtime.

Step five: Clarify what expectations others have of you

You may be lucky enough to have been given a detailed job description, but the chances are there are still large gaps in your understanding of the task and priorities, what is or isn't acceptable in the new environment, and on what criteria you will be judged by your boss, peers, customers, and others. Don't be afraid to ask a lot of questions to clarify these issues, and then be very honest with yourself. Can you meet these standards? If not, what might you need to do? Who could help, and what might the price be?

The perils of the 'new broom' syndrome

While you'll be keen to get going in your new role and make your mark, do tread carefully—at least to start with. Don't assume that your new team will welcome your style or your ideas with open arms, even if your predecessor was unpopular. Before you can count on their support and co-operation, they need to feel that they can trust you and that they respect what they've been doing previously.

Above all, don't depart too dramatically and quickly from established practice: even if you're desperate to change 'the way things are done around here', people are much less likely to throw their hands up in horror if you tackle things gradually. That doesn't mean that you do nothing, simply that you filter in new ideas and ways of working bit by bit.

Step six: Show your commitment to individual development

From your initial meetings with your team, you will know what their individual aspirations and hopes are for their jobs going forward. Follow up by setting a code of management practice that you tell all team members about, and then follow it rigorously. This code might include commitments to assess training needs, to hold regular team meetings and one-to-one sessions, to set specific goals, and to evaluate performance against these goals.

Support this code by the way you yourself behave towards team members. Make a point of appreciating extra time and effort that people put in, listen properly to what they say, and be generous in your praise of their good qualities or achievements. The point is, that by demonstrating to your team that you as their manager are on their side and will do everything in your power to support them, you will gain their trust and acceptance, and the performance of the whole team will be greatly enhanced.

Step seven: Lead by example

A good manager is also a role model, so it almost goes without saying that you must set an example for how you want your team members to behave. Lead by involving people in establishing group objectives, setting standards, and achieving deadlines, and demonstrate your own strong personal commitment to achieving the team's goals. Set an

TOP TIP

In most workplaces, there's nearly always someone who is a nightmare to work with. Before you were a manager, if you had a troublesome colleague you may have let off steam about him or her to a friend in the office. Being a boss doesn't mean you have to be a saint, clearly, but it does mean that you have to be extremely careful about what you say about colleagues and to whom. Even if you feel like screaming, don't commit any derogatory comments about a colleague to e-mail: it's all too easy to inadvertently send them to the wrong person. Also be careful about conversations you have in the office— you could be overheard. Use your common sense and, if you can, wait until you get home and unburden yourself to someone completely outside of your work life: your partner, friends, family members, or pet!

example too by maintaining high standards in your appearance and general behaviour and by establishing warm, friendly relationships.

Step eight: Take stock regularly

At the end of your first week, identify issues that need attention and make a plan for the following week. Get into the habit each week of setting aside some time for review and planning. Don't let your mistakes lead to self doubt: everyone makes them. The key thing to remember is that good managers learn from their mistakes, while bad ones repeat them.

Common mistakes

✗ You make promises that may be difficult or impossible to keep

It is very tempting, during the phase of settling in and relationship building, to make all kinds of promises to your team, boss, or customers in the interests of creating a good impression. Do remember, though, that you'll be judged on whether or not those promises are fulfilled, so be cautious about what you say you'll deliver. It's much better to under-promise and over-deliver.

✗ You make alliances based on first impressions

Common myth has it that first impressions usually turn out to be accurate, but this is often not true. Your understanding of people and circumstances may change substantially as you learn more about them—especially if you've moved company and are grateful for a friendly face in your few weeks—so don't cement yourself into new relationships that later turn out to be inappropriate or that might alienate other, potentially more useful, allies.

✗ You miss being friends with your team

This is probably the hardest part of promotion for many people: you're thrilled at the great opportunity you've earned, but know that your relationships with many people will change irrevocably. Whether you're new to just the job or the company, you need to build good relationships with your team members but also distance yourself a little from those who report to you so that you can be objective and unbiased in the way you work with them. This can be difficult when you have previously been a member of the team yourself, but, if you don't, you run the danger of being seen as a manager who has 'favourites' and of allowing your personal feelings to affect your judgment. This won't be good for your team's morale and you'll also lose much of your authority. It's probably best to be honest about how you feel with particular friends so that you are seen to maintain a professional relationship at work, and you can then keep purely social activities for outside the office.

✗ You're trapped into accepting the status quo

Whatever anyone says about 'the way things are done round here', the old ways are not always the best. Reserve your right to postpone judgment until you are thoroughly familiar with your team and your role and then, if things need changing, change them – remembering, of course, to be tactful in the way you do it.

STEPS TO SUCCESS

✔ Don't let worries about your new job get the better of you. Your skills and experience have got you this far, so keep positive and enjoy this challenge as much as you can.

✔ If you're a 'details' person, you might find it hard to let go of some tasks so that you can concentrate on the bigger picture—the goals your team, department, and company need to meet. That's exactly what you must do, though, so be ready to adjust.

✔ Research and planning will help you to make a smooth transition into your new role. Find out exactly what's expected of you and come up with a basic plan of how to make it happen.

✔ Spend time getting to know your team and listen carefully to what they have to say—they could prove to be your greatest allies.

✔ Don't overpromise. It's tempting to get people on-side by telling them exactly what they want to hear, but you'll end up backing yourself into a corner.

✔ Plan some quick wins to help you feel more in control.

✔ Tread carefully at first if you're introducing change. People's knee-jerk reaction to change tends to be negative, but, if you bring it in gradually, you'll get a less panicky response.

✔ Lead by example. You can't expect others to behave professionally if you don't.

✔ Be very careful about what you say—and to whom— about your colleagues at work, even if they're driving you mad. Use your common sense and be discreet, however angry or upset you are.

✔ Don't beat yourself up if you make mistakes. Experience is the best teacher you'll ever have.

Useful links

HR Guide:
www.hr-guide.com
HR Next:
www.hrnext.com
HR Village:
www.hrvillage.com

Building great teams

As we saw in chapter 1, one of the challenges of being a new manager is getting to grips with the fact that you're now running a team, rather than just being part of one.

A good manager possesses authority along with strong communication skills and a lightness of touch that draws the various personalities present in the team together so that they work well towards achieving their joint goals. This may seem like a tall order in the early days but it *is* something that can be developed through experience.

Every leader has his or her own style, and when developing a high performing team this needs to be combined with an understanding of:

- the benefits of team-building—what it can achieve and what the leader should be striving for
- team roles and dynamics—how teams work and achieve their greatest success
- the key stages of team development— what they are and how to support the team in each stage

- **the features of a successful team and team leader**
- **how to avoid potential problems and pitfalls.**

Step one: Understand what makes a good team leader

Leadership, in broad strokes, is the capacity to establish direction and motivate others towards working for a common aim. Successful teamwork depends on the team leader's ability to make sure all team members know what that aim is and what they each need to do to achieve it.

Naturally, all teams are different and have their own dynamic, and all leaders develop their own style for forming, developing, and leading them, but there are some general characteristics of a good team leader. For a team to work, it's essential that all members are committed, so leaders must be supportive, enthusiastic, and motivating people to work with. They must organise and communicate well in order to co-ordinate team efforts both *within* the team and with others *outside* the team. During difficult or stressful times, team leaders need to be approachable, good listeners who can offer feedback and advice. Turn to chapter 3 for more advice on ways to boost your leadership skills.

What are the features of a good team?

It goes without saying that successful teams are ones in which people don't waste time trying to achieve success at the expense of others. Instead, they work at understanding each other, and communicate honestly and openly. They're committed to the team's success and are respectful and supportive of each other, sharing information and experience.

Conflict is unavoidable in most work situations, but a good team will work through it and reach an understanding by generating new ideas. A good team also acknowledges the role of the leader and understands when he or she needs to act and make a decision (in an emergency, for example, or if there is a major problem or disagreement). See Step six for more advice on this issue.

Step two: Focus on the work

For anyone interested in productive teamwork, it's often better to start with the work rather than the team. First of all, think about whether the job in hand really does need a team to tackle it. Some types of work, such as repetitive or unskilled tasks and, at the other extreme, specialist activities, are best performed by loners. Rounding up such people and forcing them to work as part of a team risks producing a double disadvantage: their personal productivity falls and they feel that their privacy has been invaded.

While it's currently popular to strive for such an 'all inclusive' approach in the workplace—and some people argue that isolated workers need a social dimension to their work—there are often few benefits from forcing this set-up on someone. Introverts need work suitable for introverts, while extroverts need work appropriate to extroverts.

Step three: Help the team succeed

The team approach for organising work depends on empowerment–that is, making sure that each person is allowed to perform to the best of his or her abilities. This relies on trust, the confidence that a manager places on the qualities and calibre of the employees. It also depends on how well members of a group have developed an understanding of each other's strengths and weaknesses. That's why, if your budget allows, training in teamwork is so important and why it helps to understand the language of team roles.

TOP TIP

As a team leader, remember that you have to allow team members the freedom to do what their role entails—empower them. Give them all the information they need and set boundaries to make sure that things happen.

Communicating clearly

One essential part of working well with your team is communicating clearly with them. It is also useful to know that different people absorb information in different ways. So, when you're communicating, it's important to do so in a manner that gets through to as many people as possible.

Research into learning styles during the 1970s established that people fall into four main categories:

1 **'Why?' people:** who want all the reasons for doing something
2 **'What?' people:** who want all the facts about it
3 **'How?' people:** who want only the information they need to get on and do it
4 **'What if?' people:** who are more interested in the consequences of doing it.

It was also found that if any of these kinds of people don't get the type of information they naturally prefer they tend to switch off. So every presentation, information booklet, team talk, or other communication device you use has a much better chance of being heard and absorbed by everyone in your team if it contains all four elements.

TOP TIP

It's also worth remembering a very useful concept known as the 'three times convincer'. This is based on the fact that 80 per cent of people need to hear a message three times before they buy into it; 15 per cent need to hear it five times, and five per cent up to 25 times! Bearing this in mind, then, messages should be restated at least three times, preferably in different forms, with a few days between each time. It's also a good plan to vary the message so that it's saying the same thing in three different ways.

Step four: Reward teams at the right time

All teams need to be assessed, but how should it be done so that it's positive and constructive? One way is to set objectives for teams and judge how well these have been met. This view is popular in the 'top-down' school of management, where, as the name would suggest, senior managers make all the decisions and these are then passed down through the ranks to employees. In larger organisations, this approach is given added impetus by performance-related bonuses.

The argument is that teams need fixed incentives to perform

well, an assumption linked with the opposite view that without such an incentive a team won't perform well. This approach can, however, backfire. Success in meeting given criteria depends partly on circumstances and contingencies, and may not be a completely honest reflection of effort or skill. Also, objectives may be too easy to reach, or too difficult. In the end, people may focus more on the shortcomings of the incentive than on the work they're doing. Retrospective awards for good team performance (that is, given once the project is complete) are better received than prospective rewards for teams given set targets.

Step five: Stick to the essentials of effective teamworking

Again, start with the work and think about whether it really calls for a team at all. If you do decide that a team is the best way to tackle a task, work out who will be doing what; also, decide which remaining tasks can be assigned to others and make sure those involved know the responsibility for completing those tasks rests with them.

TOP TIP
If possible, train your team so that it plays to the best strengths of its individual players. Make sure each person is allowed to develop ownership, pride, and maximum commitment to the team's responsibilities. One way you

---

can do this as team leader is by delegating effectively (see chapter 5). Finally, understand what motivates the team—what gives it its momentum?

Step six: Resolve conflict

Whatever your line of work, conflict is bound to arise from time to time. Complex projects in particular are breeding grounds for conflict because they are temporary situations and tend to change continually. Unresolved conflict can be very destructive, so it needs to be tackled immediately. Here's how:

1 Recognise conflict
Conflict can be either overt (clearly visible and stemming from an easily identifiable cause) or covert (bubbling under the surface, from a less obvious or apparently unrelated cause).

2 Monitor the climate
Look out for early warning signals so that you can deal with the conflict quickly, before it gets out of hand. Early action saves time and stress later.

3 Research the situation
Spend time finding out the root cause of the conflict, who is involved, and what the potential effects are. Putting yourself

in other people's shoes will enable you to understand and
empathise better.

4 Plan your approach

Encourage everyone involved to be open and understanding
in the way they interact with others. It might be a good idea
to ask people to write down their thoughts and feelings, so
that they can express themselves logically and
constructively.

5 Tackle the issue

✔ Give everyone a chance to express their point of view.

✔ Avoid fight or flight: fighting back will only make the
situation worse, while running away from the situation
will show that you don't feel up to resolving the situation,
and it may lead to a loss of respect.

✔ Remember to be assertive. Becoming aggressive will get
you nowhere, but being passive won't achieve anything
either.

✔ Acknowledge the views and rights of all parties.

✔ Encourage those involved to come up with their own
solution—if they've created the solution, they are more
likely to buy into it.

✔ Suggest a constructive way forward.

Common mistakes

✗ You misunderstand people

While it's obviously crucial that you understand the nature of the work being undertaken, you also need to be aware of the skills, experience, and approach of those doing the work. Taking account of people's strengths, motivations, and working patterns can certainly help to build or break teams.

✗ You don't understand teams and what they need to succeed

Don't become too glib about the terminology — 'team' and 'teamwork' too easily become meaningless words, so make sure you're not bandying about terms that you don't really understand. Remember to spend time evaluating whether you really need a team to complete a given task before you begin the project, and, if you do go ahead, bear in mind that not everyone flourishes in a team — some people will need more support than others.

STEPS TO SUCCESS

✔ Understand what makes a good team leader. You need to establish direction, communicate your team's goals clearly to them, and then motivate everyone towards achieving them.

✔ Focus on the work at first, rather than the team.

✔ Help the team succeed by communicating effectively and understanding that you'll need to amend your approach depending on who you're talking to.

✔ Reward teams at the right time.

✔ Stick to the essentials: think about whether the whole team needs to be involved in a project at once, if at all; work out who will be doing what and when; monitor progress and offer support as necessary.

✔ If conflict arises, as it is bound to from time to time, act quickly to resolve it rather than let it fester unchecked.

Useful link

Belbin Associates:
www.belbin.com

Developing your leadership skills

Part of being a good team leader is, of course, knowing how to lead. There are rafts of heavyweight management tomes about this very topic, but a lot of it boils down to common sense. In this chapter we'll discuss practical ways to help boost your confidence about this part of your new job.

There are many myths about leaders—'leaders are born and not made' being a prime example. It *is* true that some people are naturally better suited to leadership roles than others, but the good news is that the necessary skills *can* be learned. Read on to find out how.

Step one: Understand that there are different types of leader

As you'd imagine, there are as many different types of leadership styles as there are personalities. For example, think of three shepherds.

- The first opens the gate and walks through, allowing the flock to follow—this shepherd **leads from the front**.

- Another stands behind the sheep and pushes or guides them through, demonstrating a **supportive leadership style**.
- The third moves from front to back and sometimes to the middle of the flock, demonstrating an **interactive leadership style**.

TOP TIP
Flexibility is key to good management. For leaders to exist, there must be followers, and the needs of followers change depending on the context. Knowing how to apply different leadership styles can help you to respond equally effectively in many different kinds of situations.

Another school of thought recognises four leadership styles:

- directive
- process-based
- creative
- facilitative

Each one is related to a personality trait. Being more relaxed doesn't necessarily mean you can't be a leader—in fact, it's a positive boon in some circumstances—it just means that you have a natural tendency towards a certain type of leadership. As you become more confident and practised in leadership, you may be able to learn other styles—more dominant, intuitive, or structured, for example. Try to work *with* your preferred style until you are comfortable enough to branch out.

Clearly, certain styles are suited to particular situations. For example, a structured leader is likely to succeed in a situation where process is important, such as running a complex project. The relaxed or facilitative leader may be one who manages a professional group of people, while dominant leaders may be needed in businesses where there is a real drive or need for change.

Transferring your skills between different arenas

Don't worry if you feel more comfortable in some situations than you do in others—as you gain more experience and practice, you'll see that your skills really transfer across the different strands of your working life.

For example, let's say you can command an audience easily when you make presentations, but don't know if you'll be able to do the same with the team you've just started managing.

Commanding an audience is a great skill, and many leaders have it, but it's not the sole requirement. Leaders also need to be problem-solvers and have originality and flair, confidence and self-knowledge, strong interpersonal skills, the ability to listen, vision, good organisational skills, and so on. Your ability as a speaker suggests that you're articulate and self-confident. If you possess the other qualities too, you are well on the way to being the leader your business needs.

Step two: Get some training

If the training budget in your business or organisation permits, a leadership course will help you to gain a fuller understanding of what leadership is, and, by extension, how it will work for your business. Courses usually range from business theory to developing strategy, to understanding business risk.

TOP TIP
Even if the benefits of some training are crystal-clear to you, it's no bad thing to spell them out clearly to your own boss when you ask to go on a course. A short e-mail explaining what you and the organisation gain from it will show that you are taking your new role seriously and that you're keen to take positive steps towards boosting your essential management skills. Also appeal to your boss's pocket if you can; for example, find out if you could get a discount for a group booking if other colleagues might benefit from this type of training.

Having well-developed commercial awareness and a good business education will not only give you confidence, but will also help you command respect from others in the organisation.

Step three: Build self-awareness

Your leadership style is the means by which you communicate. The more self-aware you are, the more effectively it will work for you. This means knowing:

- what you are like
- what your preferences are
- what your goals are
- how you are motivated to achieve them
- how other people perceive you and your goals

Numerous tests and questionnaires can be used to help you explore your personality and preferences; they are widely available online as well as from books, consultancies, and other sources. Surveys are also useful, and business schools have valuable data on expected leadership behaviours. You can combine information from all these sources to establish a benchmark for yourself.

Step four: Use it or lose it

Some leadership positions require you to set the objectives for others to follow. In these situations, scheduling, consultation, and the team building discussed in chapter 2 are essential to success.

Leaders often need to work as intermediaries between two groups—those wanting the results (boards, investors, and so on), and those who will deliver them. Establish good communication channels with both parties that allow everyone to have the information they need at the right time.

The nature of the team you work with depends very much on your organisation and the type of work you do. You could, for example, work with one small 'core' team all the time, or you could need to build different teams for each different project you work on, selecting from across the business key people with the right skills to tackle the task at hand.

If you need to put a team together from scratch, try to select a group of people that contains a good balance of competent managers and energetic, loyal team members. Teams need consistent, positive energy levels to sustain momentum, so it's critical that you choose a team based on the mix of talent required, rather than on friendships or office politics.

If you are trying out new systems or approaches, do surround yourself with the right people, create a framework for support, and document the process so you can later evaluate what you have done.

Common mistakes

✗ You mirror other leaders too closely

People new to leadership roles may try to copy a leader they respect, because the person provides an easy model. This is understandable if you're feeling a little unsure of yourself in a new role, but you do run the risk of creating a false impression of what you are *really* like, or, worse, of making yourself look foolish for trying to mimic a style that's incompatible with your own personality. Good—and genuine—leadership comes from within. Rather than follow someone else's style slavishly, understand what it is you respect in the other leader and think about how you can best display that attribute. If it doesn't work, don't be afraid to try a new approach.

✗ You don't work at it

Many people hope that they have natural leadership skills, and accept leadership positions without proper training or mental adjustment. This sink-or-swim approach works sometimes, but not always! You're much more likely to be successful if you build up leadership skills, increase your self-awareness, and evaluate what you do.

STEPS TO SUCCESS

✔ Try to be your own person. By all means observe good leaders in action and learn what you can from them, but don't mimic them. Be yourself, but get the training you need to take your skills to the next level.

✔ Remember the importance of context. There are many different management styles to suit a variety of occasions. Be flexible and be prepared to change your style depending on what you need to do and who you're working with at the time.

✔ Don't be afraid to ask for advice. We don't wake up in the morning instinctively knowing how to deal with every tricky situation we might come across at work, so do ask for help if you need it. The advice of your manager, mentor, or a trusted colleague, coupled with your own thoughts about how best to approach a situation, will help you as you build your own 'brand' of leadership.

✔ Give yourself a chance. Your first few months in a new job, especially one with management responsibilities, can be challenging. Don't get too downhearted if things don't go to plan: reflect on them, draw out the lessons to be learned and act on them as appropriate, and then move on.

Useful links

Management First (Emerald):
www.managementfirst.com/experts/leadership.htm
Entrepreneur.com:
www.entrepreneur.com
The Leadership Trust:
www.leadership.co.uk
University of Exeter, Centre for Leadership Development:
www.ex.ac.uk/leadership

Communicating assertively in the workplace

Part of the challenge of any new job—and of a new managerial position in particular—is that you start having to deal with a wider range of people, some of whom may be easier to work with than others.

If you're naturally a shy person or someone who feels unsettled by people who adopt a confrontational approach to work, you might find that you need some help when it comes to making your voice heard or dealing with difficult people. Learning how to communicate with others more assertively could be just what you need.

Assertiveness is an approach to communication that honours your choices as well as those of the person you are communicating with. It's not about being aggressive and steamrollering your colleague into submission—in fact, it's about seeking and exchanging opinions, developing a full understanding of the issues, and negotiating a win-win situation, one that everyone can benefit from.

Step one: Choose the right approach

Becoming assertive is all about making choices that meet your needs and the needs of the situation. Sometimes it is appropriate to be passive: if you're facing a snarling dog, for example, you might not want to provoke an attack by looking for a win-win situation! There may be other occasions when a more bracing approach is the answer. It may feel as though you're being aggressive, but you're actually displaying assertive behaviour, as *you*, rather than other people or situations, are in control of how you react.

After a lifetime of being the way they are, some people are daunted by the prospect of change. But, if you don't change what you do, you'll never change what you get. All it takes to change is a decision. Once you've made that decision, you'll naturally observe yourself in situations, notice what you do and don't do well, and then you can try out new kinds of behaviour to see what works for you .

TOP TIP

If you feel you need some formal training, look into some specially tailored courses so that you can try out some approaches before taking on a colleague or manager in a 'live' situation. This sort of thing takes practice, so don't pressurise yourself even more by thinking you'll 'just know' what to do—get some help if you need it .

Step two: Project a positive image

✔ Use 'winning' language. Rather than saying 'I always come off worst!', say 'I've learned a great deal from doing lots of different things in my career. I'm now ready to move on and give my new job all I've got'. This is the beginning of taking control in your life.

✔ Visualise what you wish to become, make the image as real as possible, and feel the sensation of being in control. Perhaps there have been moments in your life when you naturally felt like this, a time when you have excelled. Recapture that moment and 'live' it again. Imagine how it would be if you felt like that in other areas of your life. Determine to make this your goal and recall this powerful image or feeling when you are getting disheartened. It will re-energise you and keep you on track.

TOP TIP

If you're not very tall, it's easy to think you can't have presence because people will overlook you. Many successful people in all areas of life are physically quite small, though. Adopting an assertive communication style and body language has the effect of making you look more imposing. Assume you have impact, visualise it, feel it, breathe it .

Step three: Encourage others to take you seriously

As well as doing all you can to help yourself in terms of what you say and how you say it, you need to get other people to 'buy into' your new approach to communicating at work. You can do this through non-verbal as well as verbal communication.

✔ If someone is talking over you and you are finding it difficult to get a word in edgeways, you can hold up your hand to signal 'stop' as you begin to speak. 'I hear what you are saying but I would like to put forward an alternative viewpoint . . . '

✔ Always take responsibility for your communication. Use the 'I' word. 'I would like . . . ', 'I don't agree . . . ', 'I am uncomfortable with this . . . '

✔ Being aware of non-verbal communication signals can also help you build rapport. If you mirror what others are doing when they are communicating with you, it will help you to get a sense of where they are coming from and how to respond in the most helpful way.

TOP TIP
Until you get used to being assertive, you may find it hard to say 'no' to people. One useful technique is to say, 'I'd like to think about this first. I'll get back to you shortly.' Giving yourself time and space to rehearse your response can be really helpful.

Step four: Use positive body language

✔ Stand tall, breathe deeply, and look people in the eye when you speak to them.

✔ Instead of anticipating the negative outcome, expect something positive.

✔ Listen actively to the other party and try putting yourself in their shoes so that you have a better chance of seeking the solution that works for you both.

✔ Inquire about their thoughts and feelings by using 'open' questions, that allow them to give you a full response rather than just 'yes' or 'no'. Examples include: 'Tell me more about why . . . ', 'How do you see this working out?', and so on.

✔ Don't let people talk down to you when you're sitting down. If they're standing, stand up too!

Step five: Recognise different communication styles

There are four types of communication style:

- **aggressive**—where you win and everyone else loses
- **passive**—where you lose and everyone else wins
- **passive/aggressive**—where you lose and do everything you can (without being too obvious) to make others lose too
- **assertive**—where everyone wins

Remember that people communicate in a variety of ways. Your assertiveness, then, needs to be sensitive to a range of possible responses. Here are some tips on how to deal with the different communication styles outlined above:

✔ **Passive/aggressive people**. If you are dealing with someone behaving in a passive/aggressive manner, you can handle it by exposing what he or she is doing. 'I get the feeling you are not happy about this decision' or 'It appears you have something to say on this; would you like to share your views now?' In this way, they either have to deny their passive/aggressive stance or they have to disclose their motivations. Either way, you are left in the driving seat.

✔ **Passive people**. If you are dealing with a passive person, rather than let them be silent, encourage them to contribute so that they can't put the blame for their disquiet on someone else.

✔ **Aggressive people**. The aggressive communicator may need confronting, but do it carefully; you don't want things to escalate out of control. Using the 'I'd like to think about it first' technique is often useful in this instance. The main thing to remember is that you have equal rights to everyone else that need to be taken into account, including the right to say 'no'. Remember this when you are feeling badgered or defeated by someone.

Conflict is notorious for bringing out aggression in people. However, it is still possible to be assertive in this context. You may need to show that you are taking them seriously by reflecting their energy. To do this, you could raise your voice to match the volume of theirs, then bring the volume down as you start to explore what would lead to a win-win solution. 'I CAN SEE THAT YOU ARE UPSET and I would feel exactly the same if I were you . . . however . . . ' Then you can establish the desired outcome for both of you.

If you become more assertive, people won't necessarily think that you have become more aggressive. Be responsive to their communication styles, and their needs will be met too. All that will happen is that your communication style becomes more effective.

Common mistakes

✗ You go too far at first

Many people find that they go too far when they start to practise being assertive and end up acting aggressively by accident. Remember that you are looking for a win-win, not a you-win-and-they-lose, situation. Take your time. Observe yourself in action, practise, and ask for feedback from trusted friends or colleagues as and when you need it.

✗ Others react negatively to your assertiveness

Your friends and family will be used to you the way you were, not the way you want to become and some of them may try to make things difficult for you. With your new assertive behaviour, however, this won't be possible unless you actively allow it to happen. If you find yourself in a situation like this, try explaining what you are trying to do and ask for their support. If they are not prepared to help you, think long and hard about whether they're really the right friends for you.

STEPS TO SUCCESS

✔ Try to avoid feeling resentful—if you are feeling 'put upon', act on it!

✔ Remember that sometimes passivity is the best approach. Don't mistake aggressiveness for assertiveness!

✔ Speaking positively and using positive body language will encourage others to take you seriously.

✔ It is important to listen carefully to other people's opinions so that you are clear about which points you differ on and which points you agree upon.

✔ Try your techniques out in a safe environment until you feel comfortable with them.

✔ Build up a toolkit of assertive techniques and responses that have worked for you in the past and reuse them.

Useful links

Assertiveness tip sheet, Tufts University:
www.tufts.edu/hr/tips/assert.html
The Oak Tree Counseling Self-Help Assertiveness Quiz:
www.oaktreecounseling.com

Delegating without guilt

Now that you have a team working for you, you need to get to grips with delegation. It's a key skill to develop. Delegation isn't about giving tasks to others because you can't be bothered to do them yourself—it *is* about getting a particular job done, clearly, but it's also about encouraging people to learn new skills and reach their potential, all of which helps a business to grow.

For many of us, it seems to be a natural tendency to want to be in control of everything. We find it difficult to let go of things we know we can do well ourselves. If you want to be a successful manager, though—and preserve your own sanity—that's exactly what you must do.

Step one: Don't fight it!

Some people do genuinely find it difficult to delegate, for a variety of reasons. Often, it seems quicker to perform the task yourself rather than to bother to explain it to somebody else and then correct his or her mistakes. You might worry that the person will make a bit of a hash of it and it'll take a long time to put right the mistakes they make. On the other hand, you may feel threatened by the competence of a person who is quick on the uptake and does well. You might worry that the employee may take over the role of being the person the rest of the staff goes to with their problems. They may even find something wrong with the way *you* do things.

If you lack confidence, you may find it hard to give instructions and you'll put off delegating. If you do delegate and problems arise because the employee fails to do what you've asked him or her to do, you may doubt your own ability to confront the person about his or her actions. If staff have been given increased responsibilities and have done well, you may not be confident of being able to reward them sufficiently. You might even be reluctant to delegate tasks that you think are too dull.

Finally, you may realise that delegation is necessary, but you don't know where to start or how to go about it. You need some kind of method to follow. The following paragraphs will help put you on the right track.

Step two: Understand how delegation can help you

Delegation offers many benefits:

✔ it allows you to concentrate on the things you do best

✔ it gives you the time and space to tackle more interesting and challenging tasks

✔ you'll be less likely to put off making key decisions

✔ you'll be much more effective overall.

Your team will benefit too; everyone needs new challenges, and, by delegating to them, you'll be able to test their ability in a range of areas and increase their contribution to the business. They'll be able to take quick decisions themselves and develop a better understanding of the details involved in the process. In short, good delegation can make everyone more productive.

It's all too tempting to withdraw into 'essential' tasks and not develop relations with your team. The bottom line, though, is that it's wasteful for senior staff to be paid a lot of money for doing low-value work, and passing tasks down the line is essential if other people are to develop.

TOP TIP
Delegation doesn't make things easier—there will always be other challenges—but it does make things more efficient and effective. Essentially, it represents a more interactive way of working with a team of people, and it involves instruction, training, and development. The results will be well worth the time and effort you invest in doing it properly.

Step three: Know when to delegate— and what

Delegation is such an important part of successful management that you should actively look for opportunities to do it. If you have too much work to do, or if you don't have enough time to devote to important tasks, delegate. When it's clear that certain staff need to develop, particularly new employees, or when an employee clearly has the skills needed to perform a specific task, delegate.

Start with any routine administrative tasks that take up too much of your time. There are likely to be many small everyday jobs which you've always done. You may even enjoy doing them, but they're not a good use of your time. Review these small jobs and delegate as many of them as you can. Being your company's point of contact for a particular person or organisation may well be important, but can also be time-consuming—this is an excellent task to delegate.

On a larger scale, delegate projects that it makes sense for one person to handle; this will be a good test of how the person manages and co-ordinates the project. Give the person something he or she has every chance of completing successfully, rather than an impossible task at which others have failed and which may well prove a negative experience for the person concerned.

TOP TIP
Make an effort to delegate tasks for which a
particular team member has a special
aptitude. For example, if you have a partner
company overseas, make someone with good
language skills the new point of contact. He or
she will enjoy the chance to use their
languages, and colleagues overseas will
appreciate the fact that someone is taking
the trouble to speak to them in their
own language.

Who should I delegate to?

Make sure you understand the people you're delegating
to. They must have the skills and ability—or at least the
potential—to develop into the roles you have in mind, and
must be people you can trust. Test them out first with a
few small jobs so that you can gauge their strengths and
weaknesses. Also make sure that the employee is
available for the assignment—the last thing you want to
do is put too much pressure on your most effective team
members. Aim to share the delegation among as many
employees as possible, so think about the possibility of
assigning a task to two or more people.

Step four: Be positive

Think positively: you have the right to delegate and, frankly, you must delegate. You won't get it 100% right the first time, but you will improve with experience. Be as decisive as you can, and, if you need to improve your assertiveness skills, consider attending a course or reading one of the many books on the subject. A positive approach will also give your team members confidence in themselves, and they need to feel that you believe in them.

If you expect efficiency from the person you delegate to, you need to organise yourself first. If there's no overall plan of what's going on, it'll be hard to identify, schedule, and evaluate the work being delegated. Prepare before seeing

---

TOP TIP

Use your common sense about how much detail or how many instructions you give about the task to be done. Depending on the type of job that needs to be done, you may not be able to be very detailed at all—if the task is a creative one, for example, you'll need to give the person you're delegating to some leeway so that they can test out a few different approaches. If the task to be done is urgent and critical, though, it's essential that you're as specific as possible.

---

the person (but don't use this as a ploy to delay!). Assess the task, decide how much responsibility the person will have, and keep an eye on progress.

Step five: Discuss the task to be delegated

When you meet the person or people you're delegating to, discuss the tasks and the problems in plenty of detail, and explain fully what's expected of them. It's crucial to give people precise objectives, but encourage them to seek these out themselves by letting them ask you questions and participate in setting the parameters. They need to understand why they're doing the task and where it fits into the scheme of things. Ask them how they'll go about it, and discuss their plan and the support they might need.

Step six: Set targets and offer support if necessary

Once you've discussed the details of the job to be done, agree some targets with your colleague and schedule some deadlines into your diaries. Summarise what has been agreed and take notes about what the person is required to do so that everyone is clear—sending a brief summary e-mail so that you both have a record of what's decided is a good idea.

How much support you offer and give will very much depend on the person and your relationship with them. In the early stages you might want to work with him or her and to share certain tasks, but you'll be able to back off more as your understanding of the person's abilities increases. Encourage people to come back to you if they have any problems—while it's important to let them get on with things, you should be accessible if anyone has a problem or the situation changes. If someone needs to check something with you, try to get it back to him or her quickly. Don't interfere or criticise if things are going according to plan, though, as you'll sap their confidence.

Monitoring progress is vital. It's all too easy to forget all about the task until the completion date, but in the meantime all sorts of things could have gone wrong. When you're planning the task, build in as much time as you can to review progress. If more problems were expected to arise and nothing has been heard, check with the team member that all is well. Schedule some regular update meetings with the person and be flexible enough to revise deadlines and objectives as the situation changes.

Step seven: Look at how it went

When a task is complete, give praise, and review how things went. If an employee's responsibilities are increased as the result of a job well done, make sure as far as you can that he or she receives fair rewards for it. Make a note of what the person has achieved when it comes round to appraisals or general feedback sessions: when it comes to making a case for your team member to have a salary increase, all of this will help you to build a stronger argument in his or her favour.

On the other hand, if your team member has found the task delegated particularly challenging, or hasn't been able to deliver in the way you'd expected, discuss it with them, find out what went wrong, and aim to resolve problems in the future. Listen carefully to what they have to say and try to see the bigger picture: did he or she need more time or support, or an extra budget? What would help him or her to handle that task differently next time?

Common mistakes

✗ You think you 'haven't got time' to delegate

This is very common reaction among people who are new to delegating, but try not to fall into this trap. It's particularly tempting to think like this if you're new to a job, as you may feel that others will think you can't cope if you don't do everything yourself. In fact, delegating less important or very time-consuming tasks to your new team is one of the best things you can do. It will free you up to concentrate on the big jobs to be done, and make your team feel that you trust them and want to involve them in what you're doing.

✗ You expect people to do things like you do

Managers often criticise the way things are done because it isn't the way they would have done it themselves. This is unreasonable and unfair. We all work in different ways, so try to concentrate on the results rather than the methods used to obtain them.

✗ You don't give people a chance

If you're giving someone something new to do, you must be patient. It'll take time for employees to develop new skills, but it's time that will pay off in the end. Have faith in the people around you.

✗ You delegate responsibility without authority

It's unfair to expect results from someone who has one hand tied behind his or her back. If you're going to delegate responsibilities, make sure that everyone else involved with this task knows this too. Make clear that the person you've delegated to is the contact person for all matters related to that task and that you've given them the authority to get on with doing the job well.

STEPS TO SUCCESS

✔ Take every opportunity you can to delegate tasks to your team. You will all benefit from it.

✔ When you're delegating a task, take some time to pick

the right person for it, rather than hand out work randomly to the next person who passes your desk. If at all possible, tailor the tasks you delegate to people with the right skills, or those who have the potential to develop them.

✔ When you're discussing a task with the person who will be taking charge of it, give as much information as you can about what you are expecting, the deadline, and any other relevant information. Encourage your team member to ask as many questions as they need in order to feel confident about it.

✔ Be ready to answer any extra queries as and when they come up. It's important to offer support while at the same time letting the other person get on with the job.

✔ Don't interfere if things are going well!

✔ When the task is over, review it with the team member, offering praise, feedback, and learning points as appropriate. Make a note of successes and let your own managers know of other people's successes.

Useful link

Mind Tools:
www.mindtools.com

Giving and receiving feedback positively

As part of your new job, you'll need to get to grips with the idea of *giving* feedback to others on their performance—normally as part of a performance appraisal—as well as receiving it about your own. Most people dread even the idea of it and assume that the experience will be a negative and uncomfortable one.

It doesn't have to be like that, though—feedback is, in fact, a gift. If you're giving feedback, your main motivation is usually to see people change their behaviour for the better or to help them to make the most of their potential. Feedback is rarely given maliciously and it can genuinely help others to understand how they're perceived and how they can make positive changes to influence those perceptions. Perceptions are, of course, not always reality, but they're very real in their consequences, so being aware of them will help people choose whether or not to perpetuate them.

This is something to bear in mind when you're receiving feedback yourself. In the early days of a new job you can feel a bit beleaguered and not as confident as usual, so you may be more likely to take well-meaning advice as criticism. Keep your

perspective, though, and listen carefully to what is being said, rather having a knee-jerk reaction and imagining you'll never get it right: it's likely that there is lots of constructive advice you can take.

Step one: Understand the benefits

Giving and receiving feedback is one of many forms of communication that goes on every day at work. One of the reasons that it's so unappealing is that, unlike a lot of the abstract, theoretical, or downright useless information we may encounter at work, feedback is essentially extremely personal and, as a result, highly relevant to the recipient.

Unfortunately, many people feel that the most common type of feedback they receive is critical. Sadly we rarely receive as much praise as we do criticism, even though we know that someone receiving lots of positive encouragement performs much more effectively than someone who is constantly put down.

As part of your own objectives in your new role, you'll be doing yourself and your team a big favour if you can encourage in everyone a positive attitude towards the sharing of feedback. It is, without doubt, a challenge to do this, but remember that:

■ feedback is a useful way of letting people know how they're perceived by others

■ it gives recipients an opportunity to take decisions about whether or not they wish to change their behaviour and the consequences of doing that

Step two: Give feedback constructively

There's no way round it: giving feedback just isn't easy. If you've been on the receiving end of badly thought-out or tactless feedback yourself, the very thought of it may conjure up bad memories, and, if it's an area with which you're unfamiliar or uncomfortable, a feedback session can easily spiral into a critical and defensive exchange rather than be a positive and illuminating experience.

There are plenty of ways to make sure that the feedback session you're in charge of does remain positive and constructive, though. For example:

✔ **Find an appropriate venue**. Make sure that the feedback session is held in a private place and that you can speak to the recipient without being distracted or interrupted. If you have an office, turn your phone on to voicemail or ask someone to field your calls, and remember to turn off your mobile phone.

✔ **Make sure you're prepared**. Don't go 'cold' into feedback sessions of any type; it's not fair on the recipient and is likely to increase any tensions that may be there. Check that you've collected all the information you need and that you've thought through what you'd like to discuss during the meeting.

✔ **Make sure the reviewee is prepared**. If you're conducting a performance review, brief the reviewee so he or she has clear expectations on what will be taking place. Even if the reviewee has had an appraisal within the business before, it never hurts to run over timings and boundaries—some organisations prefer to hold performance appraisals and salary review meetings separately, for example.

TOP TIP

Some organisations have a standard form that all employees use to help themselves and their managers prepare for a performance review. These can include questions such as 'what do you see as your main achievements in the past year?', 'what are your personal objectives for the next twelve months?', and 'how could your manager help you more?'. Not all of these questions are pertinent to every organisation, clearly, but they may be a good starting point for your discussion.

✔ **Be positive**. Start off the session with some praise that shows you've noticed and valued particular behaviour. Remember not to use a one-size-fits-all approach in feedback sessions; you may have quite a range of personalities in the team you manage, so naturally you'll

---

need a range of approaches to suit each person's personality. That doesn't mean that you can't address an issue directly, just that you need to make sure you broach it in the right way for the person you're talking to at that moment.

✔ **Focus on behaviour, not personality**. Make sure that any feedback you give focuses on the person's behaviour (that is, something that can be changed) rather than on their character. For example, it's much more useful to ask someone if they're happy in their current position than to tell them abruptly that they're not pulling their weight! Always acknowledge a positive achievement first, so that the person you're talking to doesn't feel attacked. You can then have a discussion about what's going on, what you'd like to see happen to resolve it, and how you might help to make that happen.

TOP TIP

It's a good idea to find out whether the reviewee is willing to receive your feedback before you attempt to give it. If you think you feel defensiveness at the outset, address it directly. 'I sense that you're uncomfortable with this process. Is there anything I can do to make it easier for you?' You might want to add some reassurances also, such as 'Any comments we make today will stay within the confines of this room.'

✔ **Take responsibility**. As part of your new role, remember to speak for yourself only. Use 'I' statements rather than hiding behind the views of a colleague or group.

✔ **Ask for feedback on the way you handled the feedback session**. Even if the session was difficult, it's an opportunity to build bridges and show your willingness to learn.

✔ **Honour any agreements made during the meeting**. If you've promised some additional resources, greater involvement in a project, or some training, confirm this afterwards in writing and follow it through.

TOP TIP

Always make a point of demonstrating yourself the behaviour you wish to see from others. It's no good asking for something from others that you're not prepared to do yourself.

You can't expect people to speak to you openly about issues that concern them if you are impatient, defensive, or obstructive at every turn .

Listen!

Sometimes when you are nervous about something, you become so focused on what you want to say that

---

you don't pay enough attention to what is being said to you. This can cause all manner of problems, including knee-jerk reactions to problems that aren't really there but that you *think* you've heard. If you're nervous about giving feedback to others as part of your new job, you'll benefit greatly from practising 'active listening'. This is a technique which will improve your general communication skills but which is particularly useful when you need to absorb and react to what others are saying to you in potentially tense situations.

Active listening involves:

- concentrating on what is being said, rather than using the time to think of a retort of your own.
- acknowledging what is being said by your body language. This can include keeping good eye contact and nodding.
- emphasising that you are listening by summarising your understanding of what has been said and checking that this is what the communicator intended to convey.
- empathising with the communicator's situation. Empathy is about being able to put yourself in the other person's shoes and to imagine what things are like from their perspective.
- offering interpretations and perceptions to help move the communication forward, then listening for agreement or disagreement. This enables both

parties to start exploring the territory more openly. It is important to listen *for* at this point, which enables you to remain open to new ideas and to think positively about the other's input. Listening *against* results in your closing down to new information and automatically seeking arguments as to why something won't work.

■ questioning and probing brings forth more information and will clear up any misunderstandings about what is being said.

■ not being afraid of silence. We often feel compelled to fill silences, even when we don't really have anything to say—yet silence can be helpful in creating the space to gather thoughts and prepare for our next intervention.

Step three: Receive feedback positively

However much experience you have of working life, the prospect of getting feedback about the way you do your job can be nerve-wracking. The way we act reflects who we are to the world, and when this is criticised or questioned it can feel like an assault on our personalities. If you receive feedback that you find challenging or hard to deal with, try to put it into perspective—work is just one part of your life—and see it as information that allows you to make informed choices about how you're perceived by others.

In some circumstances, of course, the feedback (or the manner of it) may say more about the person communicating it to you than it does about you, but, whether this is the case or not, the best thing to do is to thank the person for their feedback and assure them that you'll think about it further.

TOP TIP

Do remember that you're not compelled to accept the feedback you get from others; it is, at the end of the day, their view of things. You can, of course, choose to carry on as you've been acting before, but do try to be pragmatic and see if it might be useful to bear in mind *some* elements of the feedback, even if other parts of it just don't chime with you at all.

Remember the following when you're receiving feedback:

✔ **Listen carefully**. Even if you feel under attack, try not to leap to your own defence until you've had a chance to think about and understand the feedback thoroughly. Be genuinely open to hearing what the other person is saying and try not to interrupt or jump to conclusions. The active listening techniques discussed above may be helpful to you here.

✔ **Ask questions to clarify what's being said and why**. You are completely entitled to ask for specific examples and instances of the types of behaviour that are at the root of the feedback. Let's say that the person you're speaking to thinks that you should be more vocal in meetings. So that you can adjust your approach best, ask him or her to tell you when they felt you needed to put yourself forward more. If the atmosphere is becoming tense, introduce a more positive approach by asking for examples of the behaviour they'd like to see more of.

✔ **Keep calm**. Even if you feel upset, try not to enter into an argument there and then; just accept what's being said and deal with your emotions at another time and in another place. Stay calm and focus on the rest of the feedback.

TOP TIP

As outlined above, giving feedback can be an uncomfortable experience too, and people generally don't do it unless they feel that you can benefit from their observations. Try to remain engaged throughout and don't start a 'tit for tat' exchange .

Receiving feedback doesn't mean that you can't talk to the other person about your behaviour. For example, you may want to ask if the giver has any suggestions about what you could do differently or to explain why you did things in a certain way at a certain time—the person you're speaking to may not be aware of all the pressures you were under at the time, or of the background to the issue at hand. You don't have to accept what the other person says, but asking for suggestions from them demonstrates a willingness on your part to take the feedback seriously. Round off the session by thanking the person giving you feedback for taking the time and trouble to share their perceptions with you.

Step four: Think about ways to improve the process

Honest and well-presented feedback allows people to enjoy good, open relationships. If feedback is a common feature of the way people communicate, issues aren't left to fester and grow out of all proportion—as they often can in a pressurized work environment.

Some organisations have benefited from encouraging a culture of 'instant constructive feedback', which encourages employees to address issues as they crop up, rather than to leave them to fester or develop into full-blown crises. This approach not only takes the heat out of more destructive or passive—aggressive styles of relating to others, but it can have a genuine impact on profitability, as ideas may be freely exchanged and innovative approaches discussed. If you think this would be appropriate for your workplace, why not suggest it to your own manager or raise it with your team?

Common mistakes

✗ Both parties get defensive

As people can often feel under attack in a feedback session, they can become defensive. This often happens when either or both parties believe they are right and identify strongly with their 'cause'. As a result, people are unreceptive to suggestions about ways to work differently, however useful they might be. Tense situations of this type are difficult for most people to cope with, never mind someone new to a management position, but the best thing you can do is to keep calm and to try to maintain good rapport throughout. This involves the free expression of views and a genuine desire to understand each other's perspectives.

If you hit a rough patch, take a step back for a moment and quickly summarise what you've covered and agreed on so far: this will highlight the positives and hopefully lead to more constructive discussion.

✗ You make assumptions

Jumping to conclusions about other people's values, motivations, or intentions can quickly cause relationships to deteriorate. Rather than wading in armed with only your assumptions, give the other person the chance to explain how they've been acting or feeling early in the feedback session. Ask open questions and be patient: some people take a while to 'warm up' and feel comfortable in this type of setting.

STEPS TO SUCCESS

✔ Giving and receiving feedback doesn't have to be an uncomfortable or tense experience. See feedback for what it is: a useful way of showing people how they're perceived by others.

✔ If you're giving feedback to others, give yourself plenty of time to prepare. Remember to:

- find an appropriate venue
- make sure the reviewee is prepared and knows the scope of your discussion
- be positive, and start the session off with some praise
- focus on behaviour (which can be changed) rather than personality (which is unlikely to!)
- take responsibility for what you're saying
- be sure to follow up on any agreements made in the meeting

✔ Make use of 'active listening' techniques. These will make sure that you concentrate on what is being said, rather than just wait for an opportunity to speak again yourself.

✔ When you're receiving feedback yourself, try not to take it personally. Work is just one part of your life and feedback is very rarely given maliciously. Remember to:

- listen carefully
- ask questions to clarify what is being said if you're not sure about it
- ask for specific examples so that you can see how you can do things differently next time
- keep calm, even if you feel upset; you're under no obligation to accept the feedback given to you, although it's wise to be pragmatic and to see if any (even if not all) of the points raised are useful.

Useful links

The ACTIVE REVIEWING guide:

http://reviewing.co.uk/archives/art/3_9.htm

Giving and Receiving Feedback, mapnp.org:

**www.mapnp.org/library/commskls/feedback/
feedback.htm**

personal-development.com:

www.personal-development.com/chuck/index.html

Selfhelpmagazine.com:

**www.selfhelpmagazine.com/articles/growth/
feedback.html**

Fighting back against information overload

There are many exciting aspects to a promotion—a better salary and benefits, or getting your 'dream job', for example—but one of the downsides is having to deal with a lot more information. Being copied in on more e-mails, writing extra reports, and keeping relevant notes on your staff's progress can take up a huge amount of time, and that's on top of doing your 'day job' too!

So where has all this extra information come from?

- There are many more means of instant communication and data access. Mobile phones, the Internet, voice-mail, e-mail, instant messaging, and tele- or video-conferencing have all contributed to the vast and fast flow of information.
- Despite this increased access to information, fewer people are employed to manage it. Secretaries and personal assistants have been replaced by laptops, PDAs, and BlackBerries.
- Everybody expects information much more quickly. For example, customers are getting used to completing transactions at the click

of a button, within just a few minutes. They no longer have to wait for endless copies of paperwork to pass through several pairs of hands before they can place an order.

■ Business structures have changed so that many projects are now outsourced, demanding clear and rapid communication between many groups of people at once. If your role dictates that you're involved with several projects at once, you could be deluged with information from all sides!

The problem is that we've all had to deal with this influx without any preparation, training, or time! Often, we find it difficult to process the flood of information—we feel as though we're drowning, struggling to find time for more important tasks. The good news is that there are steps you can take to keep your head above water and to concentrate on succeeding in your new role.

Step one: Understand the scale of the problem

Although information overload is a fairly recent phenomenon, it's already claimed casualties. Many of us feel that we have to keep up with the information flow in order to perform well, yet increasing amounts of time are required to help us wade through the massive amounts of data available. This time pressure is resulting in stress and, in some cases, burnout. A worldwide survey conducted by Reuters found that two thirds of managers suffer from increased tension and one third from ill health because of information overload.

What's the result?

Information overload contributes significantly to workplace stress. This is turn affects all areas of your life as it manifests itself in many ways, including increased levels of anxiety, short-term memory problems, poor concentration, and a reduction in your decision-making skills—the last thing you need when you're getting to grips with a new job. You can, though, take control of the problem and regain control of your desk

Step three: Take control of the problem

Information management, like time management, is a matter of discipline. To get on top of things, you need to set boundaries around how much time you're prepared to spend processing information.

First of all, decide what your limits are and create a personal information management system that works for you. This may be setting boundaries around the time you spend responding to e-mails, filtering them through your assistant (if you're lucky enough to have one), or responding only to those e-mails that hold high importance for you. Draw up some criteria to work out what you allow through your filter and what you want to screen out. This may mean putting priorities on your e-mails and deleting those that are low priority, returning calls only to those people you need to speak to, and only looking at a piece of data once before deciding what to do with it. If you miss something important, don't worry; if it's really that important, it'll come back to you in one way or another.

TOP TIP

Identify time-wasting information and cut it out of your day. For example, you could ask to be removed from your company's list of often unnecessary 'everyone' e-mails; request a good spam filter from the IT department; or ask for a summary of overly long minutes or reports.

Step two: Look for information efficiently

Whenever you're looking for information—when you're writing a report, for example, or researching a new market— keep the 'Pareto principle' in mind. This holds that 20% of what has been accessed probably holds 80% of the information you need. So much information is now at our disposal that anxiety about missing something prompts us to spend far too much time wading through every piece of data available.

TOP TIP

Remember that before the Internet, people used to make decisions in ambiguous situations; it was considered to be a management skill. Aim to develop your instincts along with your knowledge—both will stand you in very good stead as you progress through your career.

As part of your new, efficient approach to knowledge-seeking, find your own preferred places for accessing information and discipline yourself to go there *only*. You already know the high-quality sites for your particular field of work, so why waste time elsewhere? Failing this, you could make use of the information officers in the library of your professional body, if you have one. They're experienced at finding relevant information and can often save you a great deal of time.

Finally, look only at data that is relevant to your job, the project you're working on, or the decision you're making. Bear in mind the principles of time management, as they're just as effective for dealing with information overload. For example, surfing the Web is incredibly seductive, with each link taking you further and further into fascinating, but unnecessary, detail. Decide how much time you'll spend in each session, print the information that is relevant, and leave the rest in the ether. You often pick up all the information you need in a few hits, the remainder being less fruitful.

TOP TIP
The more specific you make your searches, the
more efficient they will be—you'll probably
pick up most of the information you need in
the first ten minutes or so.

Step four: Learn to say 'no'

Try not to be the dumping ground for information that others
don't want to wade through. This will involve being polite but
assertive and also being sensible; if you're snowed under as
it is, don't even hint at being receptive to this type of task.
Take control of what passes over your desk and decide not
to be held to ransom by a piece of information.

To give yourself some much-needed space, limit your
availability. Leave your mobile phone switched off for periods
during the day when you can be quiet and restful, or let your
voicemail field calls for you. This way you can decide who to
speak to and when to schedule the conversations. Anyone
who needs to speak to you urgently will find a way of getting
through to you.

Step five: Learn to throw things away!

Don't be a hoarder. Have the courage to throw data away or
delete files when you've exhausted their usefulness. You can

always access the same data again and when you do, it will probably have been updated.

Step six: Use some tools to help

It may seem rather self-defeating to resort to technology to solve a problem that technology produced in the first place, but there are useful electronic devices that can help alleviate information overload. BlackBerries and other similar devices are one example. They have many functions that can be accessed while travelling, making use of otherwise 'dead' time: you can read your e-mails, edit documents, plan meetings, write reports, and even read the newspaper. Any changes can be automatically transferred to your PC when you get back to the office.

Managing your inbox

What do you do with incoming messages once you've read them? If the information is important, you may want to keep it for future reference. However, hoarding all your messages in no particular order will not only slow you down when you are looking for information, but may also make your computer system unwieldy and likely to crash.

✔ Check whether your company has a policy for retaining and storing e-mails. Archiving may be essential for legal reasons, and, if there is a policy in place, you must comply with it. Your company may

have a central facility for storing or accessing archived
e-mails; so investigate with your computer officer or
helpdesk, if you have one. You'll be making their lives
easier as well!

✔ If you have a lot of important information you need to
hang on to (deals done by e-mail for example, or
sign-offs from partners), create your own filing
system. For example, you could sort messages into
folders arranged by:

- customer or supplier name
- project name
- date of receipt
- research topic

✔ Use subfolders: for example, for each project it may
be useful to subdivide everything into monthly or
yearly folders. This will also make it easier to see what
should be archived and when.

TOP TIP
**To save space in your inbox, you might want to
copy important e-mails relating to a specific
project or programme into other applications.
For example, you could create a Word
document called 'project communications', in
which all relevant e-mails or messages are**

held centrally. Everyone will then be able to access the information if you are away for any reason, and you will all be able to find what you need quickly.

Common mistakes

✗ You get bogged down in detail

Getting drawn into the detail of all the information that's available wastes a lot of time. People often fear they'll miss an essential piece of information if they don't comb through every available source, but in fact this rarely happens. Resist the temptation to scutinise every piece of information that appears on your screen or arrives on your desk.

✗ You don't prioritise

Being able to prioritise information will save you hours, and you may even find that you can delegate some of the processing to a member of your team, outlining what they should focus on and report back to you. Remember to give your colleague clear instructions and a deadline and try not to contribute to their information overload problem!

✗ You never switch off

Not being able to switch off from the need to absorb or generate information can be tiring and stressful. Blood pressure can rise, your memory suffers, and any patience you may have had can disappear altogether. Just as the body needs time to relax, so does the mind— and not just when you're asleep. Quieting the mind through techniques such as meditation or yoga has been proven to increase health, improve memory, and stimulate creativity. It has also been linked to increased productivity and a sense of wellbeing. If these techniques don't appeal, try other recuperative pursuits such as listening to music, reading, or taking gentle exercise. Anything that allows the mind to 'freewheel' will help a great deal.

STEPS TO SUCCESS

✔ Take charge of the problem by being disciplined. The longer you put it off, the worse the overload will get.

✔ Set boundaries around the amount of time you spend each day dealing with new information. For example, you could decide to check your e-mails twice a day rather than every hour—if you have an assistant, you could ask him or her to filter them for you first.

✔ Similarly, if you have an important task to complete and you're not getting enough peace and quiet in which to concentrate, put your phone on to voicemail for a few hours. If people need to speak to you about a genuinely urgent matter, they'll find a way of reaching you.

✔ Cut time-wasting information right out of your day. If you're spending an hour a day wading through junk e-mail, ask the IT department to do something about it. If you work for yourself, take some professional advice about how to combat spam.

✔ Don't end up being 'held to ransom' by pieces of paper. Clearly, you need to keep copies of important paperwork, but file them away properly as soon as they appear—the longer you leave them lurking on your desk, the less likely it is that you'll ever put them away safely. Throw away anything you genuinely don't need it.

✔ Learn to say 'no'. Don't agree to hold on to unimportant documents that no-one else will take responsibility for.

✔ Be efficient in the way you look for information as well as in the way you store it. If you know exactly what you're looking for, go to the best sources of information for it rather than search randomly. If you are researching online, remember that the first hits you get via a search engine will probably be the most useful. Once you have the information you need, stop looking and don't be tempted to click onto less-relevant (but still interesting!) sites.

Useful link

Chartered Management Institute:
www.managers.org.uk

Building your network of contacts

Everyone at work can benefit from building an excellent network of useful contacts. Business today is driven by relationships. Starting or growing a network—and marketing yourself along the way—requires you to build strong and meaningful relationships; many will be long-term and some may be extremely helpful as you settle into your new role as a manager.

Before you plunge in, ask yourself the following questions:

- Why am I networking? What's my personal or professional goal?
- What are my strengths that will help me to market myself?
- What organisations or events will be valuable places for networking?
- How much time do I want to spend on networking, and when will I do it?
- How will I know when I've been successful?

Step one: Find out more about the ideas behind networking

The more self-effacing amongst us may feel uncomfortable about the idea of networking and worry that it will appear to others that you're blatantly 'after something'. If you're one of those people, try to see the positive benefits of putting yourself 'out there'.

For example, research has shown that people who have a good network of contacts, who are involved in professional and community activities outside the normal job, and who look for opportunities to be visible are more successful in their careers and contribute more effectively to the company they work for.

TOP TIP

Once you start to build your network, you'll find that it becomes a way of life, and is something that you do all the time and instinctively. As you build professional relationships, be constantly thinking: 'What can I offer this person?', 'How can I be of help?' The more you try to be of service to others, the more people will want to do things for you.

Step two: Be clear about the purpose of your networking

There are many reasons why you might want to network and market yourself. Our main focus here is on building on your recent promotion and getting your name more widely known, but, if you're looking for a new job or even hoping to gain support for a major project, networking can help you too. Your efforts will be much more effective if you know exactly why you're building these relationships and what you hope to accomplish. Everyone has limited time, and this will help you to decide how to prioritise your networking activities.

Step three: Make a list of your strong points

When you're networking and marketing yourself, it's important to have a sense of who you are and what your strengths are. Think about:

- your special skills and abilities
- any unique knowledge you have
- experiences that other people may find valuable
- characteristics and beliefs that define who you are

Knowing your strengths will give you a confidence boost and

also help you to remember that other people will value what
you have to offer.

TOP TIP

**Never network from a position of weakness.
Networking from a position of strength — and
always having something of value to offer
others — means that people won't see you as
an annoyance. Also, try as far as you can to
begin networking *before* you need anything
from other people. People will be much more
inclined to help you if you join or create a
network to build relationships, and do what
you can to help others or the organisation
before you ask for help for yourself.**

Step four: Make a list of helpful organisations and events

Once you know your own overall goals and what you have to
offer others, you can make a start on getting to know people
who can help you.

First of all, find out about professional organisations and
events that may be helpful to you in your career or with your
project. Look for special interest groups, like those for
'entrepreneurial women', for example. Take the plunge and
get involved! When you're at professional events, like

conferences, make sure that you attend social functions, that you join people for dinner, and that you seek out volunteer opportunities. Don't hide in your room and hope that people will come and seek you out.

If you're aiming to network within your current workplace, find out whether there are any special interest groups or social groups to join. If not, start some! Do a bit of 'market research' beforehand among your colleagues, and, if they're willing to come along, ask each of them to bring someone else that the other attendees won't know—that will widen your pool of contacts. You could also look for committees to be involved in. Don't be shy about asking questions and making suggestions.

TOP TIP

If you aren't sure where to begin on this step, ask for advice from a mentor, from your boss, and from trusted colleagues. If you are naturally a shy person, try not to get paralysed by nerves, but see it as a real step in the right direction—networking could mean the difference between getting a dream job and feeling unfulfilled for ages in your current position.

Step five: Create a contact list

Keeping in mind your reasons for networking, come up with a list of all the people you know who might be of help to you. Next, prioritise the list according to who is most likely to be helpful. Think about people you've done favours for in the past who might not be of direct help but who may know someone who can be. After you've spoken to each person, ask him or her if they know of anyone else who might be able to help you. That way, your network grows larger at a stroke, and you have a personal recommendation to boot.

Step six: Create an action plan with a schedule

Take your list of organisations and events and your contact list, and put together an action plan for making connections. Schedule networking events in your diary, along with organisational meetings, conferences, and so on. If you're really determined, you could set up a timetable for making a certain number of calls per day or per week to the people on your contacts list.

Step seven: Meet up with people and attend events

It's now time to step out from behind the telephone or e-mail inbox! Meeting people and attending useful events is probably the best way of making the most of your network. Beforehand, review your list of strengths and focus again on why you're networking and marketing yourself in the first place. All of this will help you to visualise a successful outcome and thus banish any last-minute nerves or self-doubt. Be friendly and professional—but most of all, be yourself.

TOP TIP

Always spend time connecting with people on a personal level *before* you ask for their help or share your reason for networking. If you're meeting in person with someone on your contact list, always bring a gift—something they can remember you by.

Networking on the Internet

While there's no substitute for meeting people face-to-face, it's not always possible. The Internet is a valuable place to make connections and to learn fruitful information from contacts all over the world. If you

have a special interest or a special field, there is sure
to be a newsgroup or threaded bulletin board on
your topic.

Step eight: Market yourself

Marketing yourself goes hand-in-hand with building a
network, and the two can complement each other
powerfully. The strategy you use to market yourself will
depend very much on your own personal goals, but,
as a general rule, think of yourself as a brand: 'Brand
You'.

For example, when marketers are marketing a product,
they look for the 'Unique Selling Proposition' (USP),
something relevant and original that can be claimed for a
particular product or service. The USP should be able to
communicate: 'Buy our brand and get this unique
benefit'.

If you're marketing yourself, you need to use the same
principles and define who your 'customers' are and what
your USP is. Your list of strengths above should give you
some clues, but the best USPs are short and snappy,
such as 'I solve problems quickly and simply' or 'My
leadership brings out the best in others'. The people
closest to you can often give good suggestions if you
get stuck.

TOP TIP
Once you know your USP, think about ways
that you can market yourself and your unique
qualities. The key is to let people know what
you have to offer. For example, you could
design a project that uses your talents and
propose it to the right people; volunteer to
give a talk; or write an article for an in-house
or external publication that shows your skills
off to best advantage. Don't be afraid to be
visible!

Step nine: Keep an eye on your progress

It's always a good idea to keep track of your progress and of
where you are in your action plan: a notebook or simple
planner is all you need. It also helps to have someone as a
sounding board, such as a friend, a family member, your
boss, a mentor, or a professional adviser. When we feel
accountable for our actions to someone we trust, we're
much more likely to follow through. Plus it's always a great
boost to be able to celebrate your successes with someone
else.

Step ten: Always say 'thank you'

As you build your network, many people will offer you information, opportunities, and valuable contacts. In your notebook, keep track of the favours that people have done for you and make sure that you write each one a short and simple thank-you letter or e-mail. People are always more willing to help someone who has been appreciative in the past.

Common mistakes

✗ You come on too strong

Networking isn't about selling someone something they don't want. You're looking for opportunities to create a relationship where there is give and take. For networking to be successful, you absolutely have to be interested in developing a long-term connection rather than grabbing a quick answer to a problem you're facing. Remind yourself that your focus is on relationship building, not on immediate results, and not exclusively on **you**.

STEPS TO SUCCESS

✔ Understand that networking is an excellent way of building strong, long-term professional relationships that benefit everyone concerned, not just you.

✔ When you first think about networking, make sure you're absolutely clear about what you're hoping to achieve. Knowing your own goals is just as important as finding people to help you to reach them.

✔ Make a list of your strengths to remind yourself of the skills, experience, and knowledge you have to offer others.

✔ Try to build your networks before you need to ask others for help. This will show that you're interested in building helpful alliances rather than just looking out for your own interests.

✔ Put together an action plan of who you intend to contact when, and which events might be useful to attend. Keep track of your plan and your progress so that you can change tack if you need to.

✔ Think about how you can market yourself as well as network. Take a step back and see yourself as a 'brand' for a few minutes. All successful brands have USPs, which set them apart from others. What is your USP?

Useful links

City Women's Network:
www.citywomen.org
Vault:
www.vault.com

Where to find more help

How to Get the Perfect Promotion: Your Guide to Career Progression
John Lees
Maidenhead: McGraw-Hill, 2003
224pp ISBN: 0077104269
Offering sage advice to jobhunters as well as those hoping to advance within their current organisation, this book offers practical and creative help on career advancement.

I Don't Know What I Want, But I Know It's Not This: A Step-by-step Guide to Finding Gratifying Work
Julie Jansen
London: Piatkus, 2004
270pp ISBN: 0273675826
A useful resource for anyone unhappy at work. Full of exercises to assess the reader's personality and skills, this book will help people to understand their present situation and come up with ways to find the job or career they really want to embark on.

The Ultimate Guide to Successful Networking
Carole Stone
London: Vermilion 2004
176pp ISBN: 0091900255
This book is a guide to communicating more effectively in all areas of life so that confidence increases and new contacts can be made. The author overcame her own childhood shyness to become a successful radio producer.